A BUTTERFLY
IN THE WIND

Martinez Shaver

A Butterfly In The Wind

Copyright © 2024 by Martinez Shaver

ISBN: 979-8-9870144-3-1 (paperback)
ISBN: 979-8-9870144-4-8 (hardcover)
ISBN: 979-8-9870144-5-5 (eBook)

Printed in USA Published by Horizon Book Marketing

For

Melody and Harmony

Introduction

People in this world will limit you if you allow them to, so be who you are with no regard to how they feel about you. Surround yourself with like-minded people, and remember there is always time for separation. The road to success gets lonely, but it is a journey worth taking. Defy every odd that stands in your way. Feed and invest in yourself daily, and even more, invest in your children. Instill in them everything you feel they need to know in preparation for this world. Teach them the truth, and ensure they know that self-education is the best education. Invest in their future, and be the best man or woman you can be to set great examples for them. Carry yourself with honor, integrity, and confidence. Demand your respect, and never accept anything less. People treat you according to how you carry yourself, so walk like an emperor. Remain humble. Seek wisdom and knowledge in all you do, and above all, keep your faith in the Most High.

Table of Contents

Faith of A Mustard Seed

Life can be crazy,
& we battle our fights.
We smile through the day,
& we frown at night.
We laugh through the day,
& we cry at night.
But, we must pray & believe
that everything will be alright.

Rain & Inspiration

The rain is drizzling, & I just feel to release.

What's flowing through me right now is simply joy & peace.

Strictly and quickly unwinding what's underneath

As I listen to the rain, sitting in my Marvelous Tahoe

Allowing it to keep the rain shielded from me

Watching the drizzles roll down the glass in streaks

As at that moment, none of my rhymes are escaping me

The lights are out, but I'm sitting below a street light.

So I, Martinez, continue to write.

You should see the effects of the light, the rain &

the glass creating a glide of imperfect,

shining circles across the page.

Steadily writing as the previous line continues to age

This feeling is so wonderful, & it is simply me.

Living in my passion, existing in my passion, and giving you

the rhymes within is what I'll continue to be.

Seasons of Life

I believe fall is the most beautiful season.

What dies, dies. And what remains, remains.

Fall air is refreshing and relaxing.

Some things are opening up.

Others are retracting.

Gold, orange, green

& sort of red leaves,

Different vehicles; different head speeds.

Sometimes

Sometimes, a man just needs to be hugged.

Sometimes, a man just needs to cry.

Sometimes, a man just needs his woman to grab him
& hold him like a baby.

Sometimes, a man just wants to be hugged.

Sometimes, a man just wants to cry.

Sometimes, a man just wants his woman to grab him
& hold him like a baby.

Beautiful Things

Finally, I understand
what "Life is like a box of chocolates" means,
but I don't understand why I dream
the dreams I dream.
Life is good, & I appreciate the simple things.
Beauty is in the eyes of the beholder,
& I see so many beautiful things.

Just Smile

I can tell that you're down,
& I just want to lift you up.
The joy I usually feel from your
conversation is missing, and
I don't know if it's got something to do with love.
It seems like it does, but maybe I'm wrong.
Whatever it is, pretty lady, just stay strong.
I am a passionate man, a bit of a flirt.
And, I love to make women smile.
So, even if you believe I'm flirting,
maybe I just want to see you smile.

Secrets

We are actually like movies;
you never know who's watching you.
One's mind is the deepest secret;
you never know what's running through it.
Words mean nothing if they remain unspoken.
A heart is still something even if it remains broken.

What Is Love?

What is love?
I could ask myself this question 1,000 times.
And, I could answer with 1,000 things.
Then again, I could ask myself this question 1,000 times.
And, I could answer with 1,000 things.
Basically, love is what love is, and
love is what it is to you.
So, whatever you think love is,
whatever love is to you,
whatever your answer is
to the question of what is love,
that's what love is.

Toxic Love

My love for you is deeper than the oceans of blue.
I didn't know that I would fall in love when I met you.
I didn't know that we would hurt each other
the way that we did.
Though we're not together right now,
I still want you to have my kid.
Take a piece of me baby, & hold on forever.
I will run to save you in the worst of weather.

Another Chance

I once lived heartlessly,
& I constantly hurt those I loved.
I once lived heartlessly
& felt I was heard by no one,
not even from the Two above.
I once lived heartlessly
until one day I broke down.
I no longer live heartlessly
because I turned my life around.

Self-Recollection

Sometimes, I really weep about the pain I feel,

but I will never bow down and give up.

I am not Superman; my feelings get hurt.

But I roll on, and that's one thing that makes me tough.

I am who I am, and I will reach my destiny.

My heart gets cold, but I always bounce back

to reach for the best in me.

Writing is my escape.

It's my strength.

It's my advantage.

It's my soulmate.

With my pen and paper, I have plenty of dates.

Cold Truth

If I would let you peak into my mind,

could you handle what you might find?

Pain, lies, & misery of leaving my childhood behind

A boy who looked up to many men who constantly let me

down

So, I decided not to look up to any man, just so I would not get

let down.

Love Making

I've had sex with some women.

I've made love to a few.

Never have I wanted to make love to someone

as much as I want to make love to you.

Our chemistry is stupendous.

Our bond is like concrete.

Words are sometimes useless

when you could just make love to me.

And if we talk during the creating of our beautiful smell,

well little lady, isn't that just swell.

Friendship

Friendship is sacred to me,
& I stand upon my word.
Friendship is sacred to me,
& I stand behind my word.
With the wind do birds fly.
Against the wind flies some birds
With the wind do birds sometimes fly.
At other times, against the wind flies some birds.
Friendship is sacred to me,
& if I call you my friend, I mean it.
So, do not call yourself my friend
unless you truly mean it.

If I Cry

If I cry, will you cry with me?

Picture a young woman, 4 kids & no food to eat.

If I cry, will you cry with me?

Picture a teen having a baby & losing her mother at the age of 19.

If I cry, will you cry with me?

Picture a boy battling the beast of weak lungs.

He was determined to play football,

but his Mother had rather he bang symbols or beat drums.

If I cry, will you cry with me?

He had no father growing up.

But, don't cry about that. He holds no grudge,

& that's one thing that makes him tough.

If I cry, will you cry with me?

Picture your childhood being stripped away.

A kid constantly in a depressing state,

the expressions written boldly upon his face.

If I cry, will you cry with me?

His special Grandad went away.

His Great Grandad with whom he counted pennies went away.

His Great Grandmother who gave him pinwheel cookies went away.

Mindful Deceit

We act like we are animals, and we believe that we are animals because we were treated like animals. We were treated like fools. We accepted defeat, and we started to act like fools. We are killing each other and are still foolish. We are fighting the war that our true enemies want to see. We intimidate the enemy, but the enemy has finessed us to kill each other. Some of us are fighting back, but many have truly laid down like cowards.

Warring One

I write with my hand.

I assemble with my brain.

I speak from my heart when I deliver the pain.

I feel the heat from the sun.

Through the glass, I see rain.

Warring one is the definition of my name.

Cold-Hearted Truth

It's a cold-hearted world, & many are sleep.

I can't lean on many, but many count on me.

I carry aggression, but I spare many

because I'm all about peace.

I'm a blender, & I'm slicing.

So, gangrene, get away from me.

I want so much for all people around me,

but horses that don't want water aren't even drinking.

I'm so thirsty that my face is nearly sinking.

My face is nearly sinking in water because I need hydration.

Hydration, Circulation, Non-complacent, Motivation.

Still Grinding

There are many poems suppressed in the depths of my mind.
I must be successful; therefore, I am always on my grind,
mentally, physically, & even with my emotions.
I want to take trips across rivers and oceans.
I want to take flights to heights I've never been
and have big cookouts with all of my kin.
I want to go fishing with my Grandad, Montana.
Rest in peace to that red nose, Santana.

Hungry Pigeon

I don't expect anyone to understand my vision. I'm determined to eat like a hungry pigeon. Sometimes, we fail to hear the Most High because we fail to listen and worry excessively about other people's opinions. My craft is my craft, and it was made for me. I am who I am, so be who you were created to be. You can't choose my walk. You can't choose my talk. You can't spit like me nor deliver my thoughts. Pass me the ice; I'm on fire like napalm. A man is not measured by the watch on his arm. A man is not measured by the car that he drives, and a woman is not measured by what's in between her thighs. Please listen. Please take this knowledge, and stop that flexing about what's in your pockets. Stop coming at me like I am young and dumb, and listen to this passage that might leave you numb. Your mind can barely fathom what I am capable of. Rest in peace my loves in the Heaven above. I said I don't expect anyone to understand my vision. I'm determined to eat like a hungry pigeon.

Watch What You Say

Words can put you down.
Words can lift you up.
Words can make you weak.
Words can make you tough.
Words can cut like knives.
Words can feel like gunshots.
So, watch what you say.
Don't let your words get you shot.
The time in which we live is like
the Wild, Wild West.
I'm here to make a change.
Let's put ignorance to rest.

I Am Who I Am

I didn't choose this walk,
& I didn't choose this talk.
Everywhere I've been,
It was love I brought.
Honesty, I brought
Loyalty, I brought
Respect, I brought
Knowledge, I taught.

Sensitivity

There is sensitivity in every man,
whether it's his woman, or his kids.
Or, maybe it's the thought of what
he went through while serving his bid.
There is sensitivity in every man.
We've all got a weak spot
like the reality of losing a loved one,
being stabbed in the back by your partner,
or being stolen by a cheap shot.
Many men front & walk around as if,
"I'm a man; nothing bothers me,"
disloyal to actuality & that's what's really bothering.
Speaking with deepness,
& I believe I can touch any soul.
Thankful for my knowledge & optimism
because my heart used to be cold.

A Crazy World

It's a crazy world out here bra, and everybody ain't true.

Snakes are walking, but us loyal ones must keep pushing through.

Most people want something in life

that they are not even trying to get.

It's a cold-hearted world, and that's some real spit.

I believe that some people are born to be leaders,

but I don't think everyone is born to lead.

We all weep. We all cry. We all bleed.

So basically, we're all still equal,

but some people leech to others like gangrene.

And, I'm telling you that it's lethal.

We must keep our head to the sky.

We must aim high.

We must strive to be greater men

because life is passing by.

It's a crazy world out here,

but I believe it can change.

Some people improve.

Some people remain the same.

A Warrior's Struggle

Lift your head up, & keep it there.

Take a deep breath.

Inhale fresh air.

Take a knee, & pray.

Thank Elohiym for this day.

Smile for your seeds,

& teach them how to pray.

Smile for your blessings.

Have fun, & play.

Rest with peace at night as you lay.

Troy

Cooler than an autumn breeze,

but can take it there

like the ruthlessness of DMX in belly.

Respectful to others,

kind & courteous

Soul of true essence,

extremely courteous

Down like Rico in *Paid in Full*

The conversations we hold are never dull.

One of those people you can talk to about any thang

I'm glad I met this guy.

Troy is his name.

Destiny

Many times have I been
so close to giving up writing.
Then my brain begins arranging
words & messages that are so enlightening.
And, I have no choice but to spit them out.
I'd be a fool not to.
Proverbs is my favorite book,
so how can I be foolish?
I can't be.
Thank Yahuah for these messages.
It's His glory.
Don't thank me.

Life Is Beautiful

Life is beautiful though we sometimes complain.
Father, forgive me if I've ever taken your name in vein.
I thank you for my family & for my friends.
I pray to leave a legacy to & through my end.

Life

Live.
Improve.
Fulfill.
Evolve.

Love.
Intrigue.
Forgive.
Enlarge.

Streets

I love the streets,
but do the streets love me?
The streets are a positive word backwards.
L-i-v-e.
Evil are the streets, & evil was me
when I was serious about
& searching for love out in the streets.
See, I got love in these streets,
but do the streets love me?
I respect these streets,
but do the streets respect me?
I got respect in these streets,
but do the streets respect me?
I got love in these streets,
but do the streets love me?

For those in need.

Remain Humble

Why must a person be less than you
when somebody makes more money than you?
Why must a person be less than you
when someone drives a flier car than you?
Why must a person be less than you
when somebody's house is bigger than yours?
Why must a person be less than you
when some people have maids to do their chores?

My Prayer

Patience is not always easy to grasp,

& sometimes I find myself dwelling in the past.

Sometimes I smile, & sometimes I laugh

because I know my troubled days won't always last.

Sometimes I weep, & every day I pray.

Father, please take our pain away.

Father, please let it not rain today.

Father, please deliver me from my ways.

Lost Souls

Some run to the streets for acceptance
and because they think it's cool.
Some run the streets to get money
so their families can have some food.
Running the streets for fun is not a smart thing to do.
Running the streets at all is not a smart thing to do.
Many souls are lost.
Some want to be cool.
Others do what they feel they have to do.

Anger Management

It's funny how they fear us because of the stereotypes they portray.

They see us as predators while they feel like prey.

Some are even scared just to say hey.

Some even fear just what we might say.

Humble are the words that I put to this page.

I pray. I write, and I smash the rage.

When my fuse is short, it takes nothing to grasp the rage.

Still, when I am angry, I blast the page.

So still, when I am angry, I smash the rage.

I hold it right here in the palms of my hands..

..take a few deep breaths & give it up to the Man.

The Chocolate Woman

You are my moonlight when I feel dark.

You are the reason that I park.

You are my umbrella when my vision fills with rain.

You are the smile upon my face.

It's your hand that caresses me in attempt to ease my pain.

You are the attraction to my erection.

You are the match to my connection.

It's more than just a nut when you & I are sexin'.

2 to 3 times a day, passion after passion,

Moaning & groaning, heart-wrenched laughing,

Pools of sweat, chills from your spine up to your neck

Red bruises from your lips on my neck & my chest,

Scars on my back & my ribs from the nails on your hands

I'm giving you all I've got,

& you keep telling me, "Martinez, you're the man."

Conversation Rules

If conversation rules the nation,

then what's the nation without conversation?

Constantly thinking, & so it seems

that I can never get too complacent.

Forever planning. Forever striving,

& always trying to make the best of my situation.

Trying to be an activist in my community,

& some are steady hatin'.

Mama Meacham

So nice, so kind
and had the most beautiful smile you'd ever see.
She made me feel I was worth something
by showing love to me.
Her lovely short hair and her beautiful red cheeks
along with her smile were delightful
and really a sight to see.
She knew when something was wrong
and always made me feel better.
She'd give you the coat off of her back in the coldest weather.
She gave me hugs that brightened my day.
She always, always knew what to say.
I first walked into her office when I was in the 9th grade,
& on that day, she stole my heart away.
She filled it with her love and gave it back.
She'd say, "I love you, Martinez."
And, I'd say, "I love you" back.

Still Love That Could Never Be

I want you, but I can't have you.

That's why when I see you,

I never hug or grab you.

I can't even look at you

without feeling what I feel for you.

At times, I feel like I'm head over hills for you.

I often wonder if these feelings will ever change.

I get butterflies when I hear your name.

The Way It Is

They may not like me, but they respect my sense.
They respect my boldness.
They respect my confidence.
They respect my humbleness.
They respect my fight.
They respect when I address that
something is not right.

Hard Lessons

Crafty & slick
Flaw like a bad smell
But, it's a test I must withstand
for my next level to prevail.
Each injury that I take only makes me stronger
For anyone to get close, their task is much longer

Different Perspectives

Some people say life is good.

Some people say life is a female dog.

Some people don't even believe in Christ,

& I just keep it real with y'all.

Some people live life on the edge.

Some people smoke crack to get high.

I want more in life than a struggle.

I just can't live barely getting by.

Extraordinary Grind

When I decide that I must have something, it shall be mine.

Constantly, I use words that I love such as extraordinary & grind.

I'm starving, and supper is getting closer to time.

I try my best not to show this rage that I carry inside.

I demand my respect. It shall be mine.

Some think it's a game.

Yet, they do not know the time.

Some see as clear as day, but still they remain blind.

Tribute to My Friends

True friends are rare. I see it clear now.

To help others, I've steadily been holding myself down.

I wonder why won't they do the same for me.

I am steadily unfolding this beast from underneath.

Anger is poison, and I kill it often.

But because of my flaw friends,

many times lately have I almost lost it.

Hit dogs holler.

Where are my real friends at?

If you feel guilty, do me a favor.

Fall back.

Faces & Vibes

Faces & vibes coincide,

and acts are brand new at times.

Faces & vibes coincide,

and true intentions can't always hide.

Faces & vibes coincide,

so read between the lines.

Faces & vibes coincide,

and envy reveals sometimes.

Poetic Hustler

I will always be imperfect,
but I am forever striving to be greater.
At times, I want to cuddle... talk about my fears & my
struggles.
At times, I want to isolate & really focus on my hustle.
I am forever multi-tasking due to my many ambitions.
And, I am no fool to these streets.
I'm just on this poetic mission.

Confusion, Containment, & Power

Being contained is a thing of the mind,

& I am sacrificing for the grind.

My load has been heavy including my shield,

but now it is time to peel.

I poured my heart… dug deep in my soul,

& lately unleashed what my mind beholds.

I've dropped some weight… strived to move at a quicker pace.

It gets lonely, but I will succeed as long as I continue to grind &

pray.

Totally Random

I don't always do the right thing,

& I only have one life to live.

Even when I do wrong, I keep it real.

I am imperfect. I am filled with flaws.

And, I do not agree with all of man's laws.

I hate politics.

I love women.

Yes, it bothers me to lose because I love winning.

My mind is tangled & twisted up.

What's the difference between love & lust?

Some are foolish.

Some are stuck.

And, some just don't give a …

Once in A Lifetime Love

Time & time again, I fall for you
thinking that we just might be.
Because we resist what lies beneath,
our friendship doesn't exist in harmony.
A love like this is rare.
I have only come across it once.
Though I care for you as deep as the ocean,
I know I mis-show it a bunch.

17 Going on Forever

The special that you are is rare.
I even wonder if we could be soulmates.
I dream of you. I think of you.
I even fantasize about a first date.
I toss & turn through the night
wishing you were by my side.
I often imagine holding your thighs,
your hands in my chest as you ride.
Umph. Umph. Umph.
I've been waiting on you since we were 17.

Desires Unfulfilled

Longing for deep conversation
Desiring to hear inspiration
You know to keep your head up
no matter what you're facing.
I long for the same things.
At times, they are hard to find.
My mind is often bewildered,
& my eyes are sometimes blind.
I often tell myself,
"You cannot give up your grind."
"You were born for a purpose,
& it's getting closer to time."
So, you cannot give up
no matter how hard it gets.
I love you, & for you,
I wrote this real spit.

Overdue Conversations

The deepest conversations are so inspiring.

The so inspiring things are so surprising.

The so surprising things are so astonishing.

The astonishing things keep me wondering.

While wondering, I fantasize.

When I fantasize, I tend to rise.

When I rise, I want to inject.

I can't even flex; I really love sex.

But, it is deeper than what meets the eyes.

It is more so in the mind.

Due to an overdue conversation,

I gladly wrote these rhymes.

Forever Grinding

I want too much to be wasting time.

I'm serious about my grind.

I must expand my mind.

What I'm doing now, I could have been done.

So, I guess I wasted time.

But now when I awake,

I am all about my grind.

They say time is valuable.

Valuable is my mind.

I wake up just to kick knowledge

& make use of my time.

The Toughest Love

I know my people wonder
why I haven't answered the phone,
but I want them to wake up
and smell the coffee on their own.
See, I'm steadily feeding them life,
& they are steady asleep.
But, who would be there for my people
if my heart didn't beat?
See, you can feel me now,
but you don't really care.
You wouldn't be there for my people
if I had no air.
You can hear me now,
but you will probably forget what I said
by the time you are leaving.
Who would be there for my people
if my heart stopped beating?

Lady & Cool

Standing next to you conversing is a serious temptation.

It's not always easy to resist what I'm facing.

Your lips are voluptuous. I love your smile.

Your skin tone is luscious, & I know that in the bedroom

it's your style to get wild.

I'm just shy of 22, and my drive is crazy.

I'd ask you on a date if you weren't a married lady.

I know you get mad attention,

& I never wanted to seem thirsty like the rest.

However, it is a strong belief to say what's on my chest.

Please, don't be offended. I can't deny my attraction.

Standing next to you conversing is a great satisfaction.

Your height is just right because I'm not too tall.

As a matter of fact, I'm not tall at all.

You consistently encourage me, & I appreciate it.

Those olive-green pants are my absolute favorite.

Lady, if I could have you, I would do whatever I had to

satisfy.

As I've already said, my attraction, I can't deny.

When I look at you, I can't help but wonder why.

Let me hold that though.

Wait. Never mind.

Principalities

Not even on my enemies do I wish bad.
People are so flaw, & it's really sad.
On my respect, I had to cut off my own dad
& a longtime friend. Man, it's just sad.
I gave chance after chance.
I reasoned and reasoned.
Now, I'm strolling on…
walking on through my season.
I tried real hard not to be so cold,
but I've been stabbed too many times,
crossed too many times,
& sometimes, we are slowed down
from what our futures behold.

Lessons

Time is as precious as a newborn baby.

It is steadily slipping away,

& life gets crazy.

I've been molded to study human behavior

because many have tried,

& a few have played me.

Love is special like a kiss from your mother,

a kiss from your sister,

a hug from your brother.

Cool's Destiny

Flaws are beautiful just as sure as
I am my mother's son.
I've got many scars
& a story for each one.
Even when I was too dumb to see,
she saw that I was a champion.
I was born to write poetry.
From destiny, I won't run.

Mama

You gave me life, & you raised me. You sacrificed to
provide.
Away, you gave your dream. So, Mama believe that when
I get this cream,
I will bless you abundantly.
You played two roles, a father, a mother
Gave me two beautiful sisters, an amazing brother
He and I stayed fighting. You stayed whooping our tail,
but you raised us right. And, we ain't ever been to jail.
You showed us The Way, The Truth, and The Light
in attempt of saving us from ever going to hell.
You gave me life, & you raised me. You sacrificed to
provide.
Away, you gave your dream.
So, Mama believe that when I get this cream,
I will bless you abundantly.

You're the greatest, & you've made history.

Your 1st born graduated a major university.

You've got a hustler and an entrepreneur. That's me.

Your 1st son is raising his own family.

In your baby girl, you've got a beauty queen.

You blessed this world with 4 beautiful things.

You gave me life, & you raised me. You sacrificed to provide.

Away, you gave your dream. So, Mama believe that when I get this cream,

I will bless you abundantly.

Unapologetically Me

I'm the coolest. I'm the smoothest. I'm the illest
at being exactly who I am.
I'm black, & I'm bold.
You can hate me,
or you can take me as I am.

Mrs. Butterfly

You're radiant like the shine of the sun.

Seeing you made my mind run.

Your birthmark struck me like a blow,

a blow from a powerful gun.

Your butterfly made me curious

to see what else lies beneath.

As I looked at you through the glass,

I was left completely intrigued.

I noticed you in a glimpse,

& with my eyes, I froze time.

Ever since that day,

you have completely consumed my mind.

Grease on A Hotdog

Sometimes, I really wonder
am I hip to the games
that women play.
Sometimes, I think back for months
to the things that women will say.
I am a man, though some women
view me as a dog.
And, I see that some of you
are slicker than grease on a log.
Like peanut butter to jelly,
ketchup to a hotdog,
some of you are slicker
than grease on a hotdog.

Poetic Hustle

Many times in my life have I felt worthless,
but Elohiym has never failed to show me
that my life is worth it.
Many times, have I been blind to see
that even in my darkest times,
He is blessing me.
He gave me this talent. He gave me breath.
I'm bowlegged, & my knees ache.
But, I've got good health.
He woke me up today, so I'm kicking these rhymes.
I believe Pac when he said Heaven ain't hard to find.
I've got an immaculate Mother, a powerful mind.
No longer in the streets, but I'm still on my grind.
I stay on my grind. By His grace, I shine.
Mama, we gone get rich in due time.

A Rough Patch

She's still a Queen in my book.

She always will be.

I know she loves me,

though sometimes, she wants to kill me.

Never question my friendship

because we always will be.

I am true to what I believe

& my words of loyalty.

I am true to what I believe.

I am who I am.

Even if you don't like me,

I remain who I am.

Irony & Poetry

Tall, slim, & totally incredible
Sittin' here sippin', hoping I'm eligible
…to have a chance to know who you are
Your beauty inspired this poem at the bar.
I admire your voice, your smile, your soul,
your eyes, your music, & your lovely hair.
I went to Jed's with no clue that you would be there.
It's funny that I planned on being elsewhere.
Your dress was nice. Your music was tight.
Your soft high five really made my night.
Black is my favorite color, & flowers are cool.
The dress you're wearing is totally you.
I didn't plan to write this.
You didn't plan to inspire me to,
but since you did, I wrote this for you.

A Glimpse in Time

Funny how the things we want most
seem to be the things we can't have sometimes.
Beauty is the inspiration behind these rhymes.
I saw you as soon as I stepped foot into the store.
I caught your backside, & when I did, it woke up a roar.
I wanted to step to you
to say some things I never said.
Because you were taken,
I said them in my head.
I wanted to hug you,
but then I would have been
too tempted to taste your lips,
too tempted to squeeze your hips.
I knew I couldn't do that
definitely not in Wal Mart.
So, I spoke & strolled on by
with my near vague cart.

A Glimpse in Time 2

Ever since that day,
you've been running through my mind.
If I could, I would rewind
& freeze a glimpse in time.
As I've already said,
I wish you nothing but the best
from the blessings above
to the pleasures of sex,
from the bed in which you lay
to the things that make your day,
from the foods that delight your appetite
to the songs that you play,
from the hands that caress you
to the words that make you smile,
from the friends whom which you hang
to the clothes that make your style.
I can't deny my attraction to you,
& I won't even try.
I'll be a friend with a shoulder
if you shall ever need to cry.

Mud Brothers

Some things are unexplained.

Some answers are hidden.

We often fail to make the best

of the time we're given.

We weep. We cry.

We laugh, and we smile.

Funny how as an adult,

you can still feel like a helpless child.

How do I deal with things?

Sometimes, I cry.

Sometimes, repeatedly, I ask the Most High, why.

How do I deal with things when I am torn and weak?

I stress. I get depressed.

And, I drop to my knees.

Simply, I pray & hold on to my faith,

lift my head up & press on to a better day.

The sun will shine again, so keep your eyes open.

Never stop believing. Never stop hoping.

Life can be crazy, and we battle our fights.

Be strong, and believe that everything

will be alright.

A Summer Night

It was a summer night, and
he was fresh off the clock.
It had been years since
they saw each other, and
the excitement was real.
She was special to him.
She was tough like him.
That's what he loved
and hated the most.
He was adorable to her,
but also cocky.
So, he tried less & less
to brag or boast.

Anger & Poetry

Your interpretations of me mean
nothing when I'm feeling ill.
With anger and rage, it's the page I kill.
With anger I rage, it's the page I blast.
I wear my heart on my sleeves
like a house made of glass.
My honesty is brutal,
so stay away if you can't take me.
Through my most humble expressions,
I ask that you pray for me.

This Life I Live

Cool like our 44th President, confident like Ali
Passively aggressive, so do not play with me
I've given in to temptations time and time again.
Therefore, every night I ask forgiveness for my sins.
Life is short, yet, it seems long along the way.
When everyday is a struggle, over and over I pray.

22

I'm 22, and I don't even hoop everyday like I used to.

I get so stressed out with no effort at all,

and I don't even feel the same when I kick it

with my dawgs.

I'm trying to come up,

but some of my homies are still in the same place.

I never look down upon anyone,

but some of my homies look at me

like I got a new face.

I'm trying to make a change, trying not to waste my life.

I realize that turmoil in my mind is still the battle I fight.

It's like second nature to do wrong, but I want to do right.

I am my worst enemy, so I am my worst fight.

Sad to say that on my birthday, I write this.

Maybe, I've been depressed because I

haven't written down the rhymes

that my mind has kicked,

lately.

Removing the Cape

I'm trying to figure out how to be happy
because I'm so sick of being stressed and depressed.
I'm sick of people looking at me
like I got an S on my chest.
I'm so sick to the point that all I want to do is cry.
I'm sick of searching for peace and wondering why.
I'm sick of keeping it real
when games are still getting played.
I'm sick of wishing I was still in the 3rd grade
because back then I was more happy than not.
I'm so sick of the fact that I think about death a lot.

Overdue

I feel like we owe
each other a conversation,
but maybe, I just miss you.
I feel like we owe
each other a hug and a kiss,
but maybe, I just want to kiss you.
I feel like our silence is
unfair to one another,
yet maybe, I just want to speak.

Everyone Wants to Be Loved

Everyone wants to be loved, but no one wants to be hurt.

Why do people often split at the time of a child's birth?

Could it be that they realize it's not time to settle down?

Is it just that the man still wants to get around?

Everyone wants to be loved, but no one wants to be hurt.

No one wants to be played, yet, we often play others.

As men do, women play & often have distant lovers.

Everyone wants to be loved, but no one wants to be hurt.

Everyone wants to be loved, but no one wants to be hurt.

Everyone wants to be loved, but no one wants to be hurt.

Why do people often split at the time of a child's birth?

Deep in Thought

With a constantly running mind, how do I make a choice?

I know He is here, but I'm not sure if I hear His voice.

I've been going through this storm for some months now.

Though I'm still standing, it's been breaking me down.

I'm praying, and I'm seeking Him constantly

because I know He has a plan in store for me.

Should I become an officer,

or should I go to school to teach?

I could join the service, but I am not sure

if I will risk my life for my country.

Some people say they see me in politics.

Others hate that I tend to speak so bluntly.

But, that is not my problem. Of it, I don't worry.

I tend to make mistakes because I'm often in a hurry.

I try to slow down, but then I feel that I am wasting time.

If I'm a hard laborer all my life,

then I will feel like a wasted mind.

Cool Guy

How can I be free if I never run in the wind?

How can I be saved if every day I sin?

Would I make it to Heaven if I died today?

Could I meet up with Pac to play bones and spades?

…that's if Pac is really dead anyway.

Could I kick a freestyle with B-I-G?

Will they remember me when I d-i-e?

Swift

Pick that ball up, and take that shot, killer.

You know you still got it.

And, you ain't even got to sell dope,

cause that paper, you know you still 'bout it.

Go on over there and say what you want to say, bra.

Either she'll go or she won't.

She might have already checked you out, bra.

Either she wants you or she don't.

Home

People are dying left and right.
The deaths are getting closer to home.
You never know when you will awake
to find that a loved one is gone.
So, Cherish. Forgive. Love. Smile.
Have fun, and make memories
that last for a while.

Your Beautiful Flaws

Flaws are beautiful to me.

I love the gap in between your teeth.

Flaws are beautiful to me.

I like the scar on your left cheek.

Flaws are beautiful to me.

I've got many to show.

You are so beautiful to me.

I just had to let you know.

Flaws are beautiful to me.

I don't mind that you are bipolar.

Flaws are beautiful to me.

And, my attraction to you gets deeper

as we get older.

Cool Breeze

I am who I am.
No human can change me.
I make my own decisions because
the Most High gave this brain to me.
I talk to who I choose because I've got freedom of speech.
I cut off who I choose because I've got the power to
release.

Life & Rhymes

Some people like to get high just to pass time.

I just like to spit knowledge through these rhymes.

Some people like to get drunk just to pass time.

I just like to spit honesty rhyme after rhyme.

Some people like to hear music just to pass time.

I try to be more potent line after line.

Some people like to fix cars just to pass time.

And, I just like to jot down the pages of my mind.

Pondering on Reality

If I died today, who would feel for me?

If enemies shot me up, would you kill for me?

If I did not have any food to eat, my brother,

would you steal for me?

I know it's a sin. Yet, I'm asking for real.

If I was dead broke, would you lend me a Franklin bill?

I'd give it right back cause I'm a hustler, baby.

Beyond the streets, I'm a hustler, baby.

Heat

Don't tell me to get deeper
if you can't accept how deep I get.
Don't tell me to keep it real
if you can't accept that real spit.
Don't tell me to remain true if you cannot accept that you
have been wrong and done wrong just like others too.
Don't tell me to keep my head up
when you keep your head down.
Don't tell me to keep on my face a smile
when on your face you keep a frown.
Don't tell me that you're here for me,
you'd die for me, you'd kill for me
when you can't even check on or keep it real with me.

High Regards

They say I take words and make magic.

I say Yahuah gave me this talent.

They say people like me can change the world.

I say we can all make a change.

They say I'm amazing. I say we're all amazing.

They say I'm creative. I say we're all creative.

They say I'm a good person. I say we're all equal.

They say family is all we've got,

and I am my family's keeper.

But, I've got more than that.

I've got friends. I've got dreams.

I've got faith. I've got hope.

And, I believe we can make a change.

Many Blessings

May your marriage be all you expect and more.

A beautiful honeymoon on a beautiful shore

Roses and tulips for a beautiful girl

A beautiful life for the two of you in this crazy world.

May your marriage be all you expect and more.

And, may you never forget that you have a friend in me.

The Process

Remember me while I'm gone,
and if I don't return,
cherish my words.
There comes a time
when you're not a kid anymore,
not a boy or a girl,
but a man, a woman.
And, there comes a time
when you must
spread your wings
and fly like a bird.

Analyzing My Surroundings

It's 3:25 a.m., and I'm in the kitchen writing.
Hot-dogs are boiling. I'm observing my surroundings.
The dishes, the cabinets, the fridge…
And, it seems like 4 in every 7
have spent time serving a bid.
That's over 50%, and those are guys
that I grew up with.
Females, it's more like every 2 in 6.
2 out of 6, 4 out of 7
And, I just pray that
I make it to Heaven.

Further Analyzation

It's 4:07 now, and I'm still writing.

My mind is still typing.

My sleep, I'm still fighting.

My peace I'm reuniting with joy and happiness

writing page after page flowing with the wickedness.

I pause and take a break.

I'm back at 4:17.

I remember being 17.

I really miss being 17.

And, I will never, ever, ever

stop chasing my dream.

A Step Back

There are droughts in life,

sexual droughts, writing droughts, happy droughts.

At times, it's like you've lost it.

Yet, you are actually evolving.

You're getting better at it.

You're getting deeper with it.

Higher and higher, you're getting steeper with it

Your passion is greater.

Your depth is deeper.

Learning more and more while becoming more eager

You're getting bolder & bolder,

more confident in who you are.

You're even smiling more because you shine like a star.

Old Times

Place of peace
and some top paper
Elevating quickly like the movement
of an elevator
Joy, laughter, and
temporary abandonment of pain
I promise that you will
remember my name.

Fantasy in Class

Thinking of what to say
to impress you and brighten your day
Reminiscing upon my fantasies
from back in the 7th grade
Waiting to see you again
because your appearance fulfills my eyes
Hoping you'll one day tell me
that I am the apple of your eye
Thinking of how to tell you
how I really feel
Hoping you'll understand that
I am only keeping it real
Reminiscing upon my fantasies
from back in the 7th grade
Waiting for you to tell me,
"let's make a move today."

All in One

I'm a poet, a son, a brother,
a nephew, a cousin, a friend,
a man, a leader, an uncle
And, I fight with a passion
for what I believe in.
I will die for what I stand.
I will bow down to no man.
And, I will deal these words from my heart
like it's 80's crack from my hands.

Motivation

My head is to the sky.
My grind is relentless.
Growing stronger in my Faith,
determination stupendous!
On yesterday, I saw the image
of my seed for the first time.
I lit the room with a smile
like the sunshine.

Comparisons

Life is like a bag of chips.
You open it up, and it could be
crunchy and tasty,
fresh and exciting.
But, there could be one chip
that looks disgusting and frightening.
Life is like a fast car; it goes fast.
Or, a pair of roller skates
…you could definitely fall
and split your pants.
Life is like a beautiful woman
who seems nice and kind,
but that impression could transform
as time unwinds.

Match to A Flame

When we first made eye contact,
I felt like we had an attraction.
She grasped my attention so effortlessly
that I could not leave without asking.
Her skin tone was immaculate.
Her lips were beautiful too.
It seemed like she was feeling me.
I was certainly feeling her too.

Broken Hero

My friends think that I am Superman.
They come to me with their dreams,
their problems, their plans.
All they see is my strength,
and I wonder why.
Maybe, it's because they've
never saw me cry.
But, they don't know that I cry inside.
They don't know how I feel inside.
They don't know that I cry when I'm alone,
and they don't know that I have no home.

Conversations Like These

Conversation rules the nation,
& your conversation is all that.
You're fly like a plane, fresh like a new Snapback.
You're still difficult to crack. You're like a mystery puzzle.
I love your ambition. I love your hustle.
Sometimes, I reminisce about the times we had,
and the things you said that made me mad,
also, the things that made me smile.
I'm still infatuated with your miraculous style.
You once told me that we would be cute together,
but I disagree. And, I'll tell you why…
because together we would be extra fly.

That Smile

Every time I see her, she gives me that smile.

I really want to tell her how I'm feeling her style.

I've been sittin' back being extra patient.

I've been contemplating and patiently waiting.

Maybe, she's just being nice.

Maybe, I think I'm too tight.

I wonder do I ever cross her mind at night.

My kicks are tight, and my rhymes are tight.

Her long black hair is a beautiful sight.

Her skin tone is a natural tan.

I sit back, observe, and adjust my plan.

Honestly, I don't care if she has a man.

I really want to know if I stand a chance.

Deliberately, I feel like I do.

You can call me a realist cause I speak the truth.

If you say I don't, then I'm cool with that.

I'm feeling like Jeezy. The real is back.

Red Bone Beauty

I see you around, & I think you're fly.

I think I'm fly too, but I'm a humble guy.

You're beautiful like a dozen of red roses.

You're noticeable like pit bulls with red noses.

A Beautiful Lesson

You can speak wisdom to a fool,
but you can not make him take heed.
Money is not the root to all evil.
The root to all evil is greed.
Steep are my goals and aspirations,
comfortable, but sometimes impatient,
and life is moving fast, so
I strive and keep on racing.
Racing to accomplish my goals,
striving to become a better man
Always giving my thanks to Yahuah
because I know that I am in His hands.
Continuously showered with blessings,
trusting and praying to eliminate stressing.
I am extremely thankful because
life is a beautiful lesson.

The Most High Hears

I used to wonder if the Most High could hear me.

Then, one day I broke down and cried.

I used to wonder if He could hear me.

I felt like I was nothing inside.

I used to wonder if the Most High could hear me.

I wondered if I would ever do something great in life.

I used to wonder if He could hear me.

And, I used to not believe

that everything would be alright.

I used to wonder if the Most High could hear me

& why was I given life.

I used to wonder if He would forgive me

for not praying sometimes at night.

I used to wonder if the Most High could hear me,

and then I started to grow.

I used to wonder if He could hear me,

but now for sure I know.

Never Cease to Have Faith

When you send up those prayers,

you gotta have Faith.

How do you awake every day?

It is Elohiym's amazing grace.

When you send up those prayers,

you gotta have Faith.

It is He who gave you your life, your face.

When you send up those prayers,

you gotta have Faith.

It could be your body at the funeral on display.

When you send up those prayers,

you gotta have Faith.

Even when you feel He is not,

He is with you every day.

When you send up those prayers,

you gotta have Faith.

I know it gets hard,

but you must continue to pray.

Black Queen

Naturally, you are beautiful
like the waves of an ocean.
You smell so sweet
like cocoa butter lotion.
Authentic are the feelings
that you have for me.
In the depths of your eyes,
lies your love for me.

Big Fish in A Small Sea

My drive is relentless.
Success is inevitable.
From those whom I slipped away,
they might feel hysterical.
Mysterious is my mind,
and the way I combine things.
Mysterious are some dreams
like sometimes when the phone rings.
Defined not by people's opinions of me,
but exactly by who I was created to be.
As cold as the winter…as smooth as grease
On all of you, I pray for blessings and peace.
Striving continuously to become a better man,
often revising and critiquing my plan,
accepting more that some things are
just beyond my control,
remembering the lessons, I was taught
& the things I was told.

The Coldest Heart

I do not want to talk.
I want to say nothing.
My heart is like a rose bush
surrounded by thorns.
And, I promise to you
that I am not bluffing.

Ready for War

Don't play with me because I'm cruel,

and I will not allow you to defeat me.

I devised a plan to dismantle you

before you ever decided to compete with me.

I saw it from a distance lead by gut and intuition.

So ye believe, ye shall be.

We can really speak things into existence.

Missing in Action

If you ever regret me,
know that I cherished you.
I enjoyed you.
You were good to me.
And, I just hope you feel the same.

Feelings Reserved

I miss you, but I can't tell you that
because you probably miss me
and won't even tell me back.
By no means am I soft.
I'm a man about mine.
By all means, I'm a hustler.
And, I stay on my grind.
I dreamed about you last night...
woke up and you were on my mind.
Honestly, I'm tired because its been a long time.
It's been a long time that things have been like this,
one minute, we're broken
one minute, we're crisp.
Crisp like a line that is perfectly straight…
We've been in love for years but never been on a date.
You tell me that you love me, and I believe that.
You tell me you love me, and I tell you back.

The Silent Killer

When you know secrets that can be crushing,
you must put forth your all to maintain.
You take shots and blows that really hurt,
knowing all the while that you can bring the pain.
There is wisdom in understanding that
we all have different opinions,
knowledge in applying that fact.
But, if not for my morals and beliefs,
I would probably put the knife in your back.

Misery at Its Finest

It weighs on me every day.

It often slows me down.

This love thing is crazy.

It makes me smile.

It makes me frown.

Poetic Isolation

I write deepest when I am
distant from everything around me.
I write deepest when I see
past everything that surrounds me.
I write deepest when I view
the world as if I have no feelings at all.
That's when I leave it all on the page.
That's when I give my all.
I write deepest when I feel
that I am trapped inside of my mind.
I just want to live for a long time.
I just want to shine.

Miserable Ties

It was never my intention to hurt her,
but my actions repeatedly showed otherwise.
I could hear it in the way she talked to me.
I could see it when I looked in her eyes.
It was never my intention to make her feel small,
never my intention to make her feel worthless
Yet, every time I penetrated in between her thighs,
I made her feel that she was worth it.
Aggressively, I sowed into her my daily frustrations.
Lustfully, I gave her sexual pleasure.
In the end, it never felt right because I knew
that I was exploiting her most precious treasure.

Human Reflection

We all make mistakes, and we all fold.

In times of uncertainty, we must remain bold.

No heart of any man will always be cold.

Life is a process like the growth from young to old.

In our younger days, we tend to be more reckless,

thriving from events that are often electric.

As we get older, we develop more patience.

We look back and smile because

through tough times we made it.

Deeper Wounds

Time is running.
Around the world, I'm running.
Fiery conversation…
we were both gunning.
I was left with scars,
& she was too.
We shall heal and overcome
when time is due.

The Strongest Friendship

I'm often afraid of being all open
because I'm afraid that you might not catch me.
I'm tough and rugged. Yet, I do have feelings,
and sometimes, they get the best of me.
I know you want what's best for me.
I hope you pray for my strength.
At times, I feel like Superman.
At times, I want to give in.
I keep pushing because I'd feel like a coward
if I just laid down and cried.
I keep pushing because I cannot give up.
I keep pushing because of my pride.
I keep pushing because my mother told me
that I am a walking gold mine.
I keep pushing because I'm a hustler,
and I have got to stay on my grind.
You care for me, and you love me
in ways that are hard to explain.
Even through all of the pain,
we still find ways to maintain.

Grill Master

I can't even hold the tears back.

It's been a while since I had fun, and I miss that.

I'm up early in the morning trying

to make a move like 50.

Ain't no love in these streets. These streets are gritty.

I feel for my whole city.

I'm real deal crying tears,

and I expect no pity.

My heart is heavy.

My mind is racing.

Make peace with all

because time is racing.

Feelings Hard to Control

I get this overwhelming feeling that I can't shake.

At times, I don't know where to begin.

I pray that our bond won't ever break.

I love you too much just to be your friend.

I see you, and I smile,

even when physically, I don't show.

I am infatuated with your style,

and on the inside, you make me glow.

At That Moment

At that moment,
I felt like I was solely yours.
At that moment,
I fell for you all over again.
At that moment,
I embraced you like never before,
and I knew for sure that we were more than friends.
At that moment,
my arms had never felt so heavy.
At that moment,
I wished that we would not let go.
At that moment,
Sweetheart, I cried tears for you.
At that moment,
they did not show.
At that moment,
I made love to you in my soul.
At that moment,
I made love to you in my mind.
At that moment,
I fantasized that we would grow old
and that you would always, always be mine.

Summer Flame

I often catch her looking at me.

My eyes barely evade.

She nearly catches me starring at her.

I turn my head away.

Her sweet voice often makes my day.

Her smile makes me feel alive.

She always has kind words to say.

For her kindness, I would shake my pride.

Night and Day 2

I want you, but things aren't currently ideal for that.
I love to see you in a dress, but also in a Snapback.
Your style is impeccable, and your frame is too.
I wonder what it's like to be in love with you.

Wordplay

Dreams and goals to achieve greatness

Bold to every challenge and obstacle I'm facing

To succeed, I'm racing while patiently pacing

Thinking critically and digging to expand my rhymes

I'm impressively lyrical and smooth as ice.

Keep your head up; It'll be alright.

If you can feel me, let me get a like.

For everyone to feel me is not the reason I write.

If it's Snapchat, let me get a swipe.

They say you can cut once if you measure twice.

They telling me to keep spitting and to get in the studio.

I'm known as a poet everywhere that I go.

I'm known to be bold everywhere that I go.

Only be yourself.

Your qualities will show.

Camila

Instantly struck by your beauty
Even your flaws were beautiful to me.
I don't know how you feel when you look in the mirror,
but I wish you could see what I see.
One of El Elyon's most beautiful creations
Walking this world in His grace
Even in 30 years, I don't believe
I will forget your face.

Just Be Who You Are

Just be who you are wherever you go.
Your light will shine and truly glow.
For your mistakes and shortcomings,
do not be afraid to ask for help.
Use your gifts and your talents to strive for wealth
...wealth financially, wealth in love
Know that you are blessed by the Most High above.
Keep Him first, and perform good deeds.
He will provide all of your needs.

Chinana

You're beautiful like a rainbow
in the sun-setting sky.
Your smile is a gorgeous wave,
and I would hate to see you cry.
Your spirit is so sweet
like honey & tea.
I hope that you will always
be a friend to me.
Your hair is precious
like diamonds and gold.
In every sense,
you have a beautiful soul.
You look like you'll age
and never appear to grow old.
You are beautiful and sweet.
You are also bold.

Martinez Ruthless

Sometimes, I long for conversation.

At other times, I be like, "bump that."

I never imagined being where I'm currently at.

I realize that I am still stuck in my old ways

I desire a new team, but I still got these old plays.

Truthfully, I never thought my life would be like this.

Yet, I know that it's about more than women and nice kicks.

I'm good at hurting people. I'm like a danger zone.

Therefore, I accept wholeheartedly being alone.

Maybe, I will never live up to the potential that they expect me to,

but if I did nothing else, I kept it real with you.

Her Name

She was beautiful by all means, and I had to have that.

She was stunning and often made me take two steps back.

When she made love to me, I felt like nothing but a king.

She loved me even when I was foul

and even though I was mean.

She has taken me to heights and left me high as ever.

She has shielded me with her protection

from the worst of weather.

She has blessed me continuously.

Together, we take flights.

Her name is beautiful.

Her name is Life.

A Different Perspective

No one can steal your joy unless you allow them to.

Only one person can make you happy,

and that person is you.

Set your goals, and chase your dreams.

Nothing in life is as hard as it seems.

Martinez Too

I'm like the villain in the horror movie.
My smile is cunning,
and my attributes are really my flaws
viewed optimistically.

Rise & Never Fold

Often red, but yellow too

Up from the concrete like Tupac, I grew.

Beaten and broken, but reconstructed

Now, an eternal warrior is what you're stuck with.

I rise everyday from my back to my feet.

I rose up even when the pain was deep.

I've been stepped on and smushed

like a rose with no appreciation.

Thanks to that, I'm heartless in any battle I'm facin'.

I still rise like Maya Angelou…

thankful every day for the gift I hold

Driven to succeed no matter the price it costs

Still, I rose up even when I was lost.

I promise that there is not a man who can stop me.

I felt like a piece of meat

when they criticized and chopped me.

I have powered up level after level.

I'm like a rose with infinite recyclable petals.

When I say I rise, I mean I rise.

Though I've cried, you've never saw the tears in my eyes.

See, I might bend, but I never fold.

They knocked me down, but again

I rose.

Eternal Warrior

Just because all you see is my strength,
it does not mean that my burdens are light.
And, just because you never see me fold
does not mean that I don't pray
for my strength every night
because I do.

The Warrior's Star

Even a warrior needs someone to look up to,
someone to keep him going
when he wants to fight no more.
Even a warrior needs someone to wipe his tears
when he can not hold them back anymore.
Even a warrior needs someone to hold him
when all of his strength seems to be stretched thin.
Even a warrior needs someone to build him up
so that he can be ready to fight again.

Dear Melody

You came out of the womb, and I was stuck like glue

as if no one was in the room other than me and you.

When I heard you cry, you changed my world.

Elohiym had blessed me with a beautiful girl.

Your first smile melted me instantly like a torch to plastic.

If anyone ever harms you, my reaction will be drastic.

I will grind hard for you, bleed and sweat for you.

Never for any reason will I neglect you.

You are my pride. You are my joy.

For you, I humble myself day after day.

You are my laugh. You are my smile.

For you, I will always make a way.

You're a Melody from Heaven created for me.

I pray on your life prosperity and peace.

How Bad Do You Want It?

Would you rather know the truth even if it hurt,
even if the truth would make you question your worth?
Would you rather know the truth
no matter how hard it might seem
…the truth that he hates to awake
from some of his dreams?
Would you rather know the truth even if it made you cry,
even if it made you feel unfly?
Would you rather know the truth
even if it went against everything you believed in?
Would you rather know the truth
even if it meant that he was unfaithful again?

Wheat Amongst Snares

Trying to remain positive

though surrounded in an environment

filled with negativity

Most often, it does not,

but sometimes, it gets to me

Stuck right now in between

two hard places

Not searching for new

and attempting to elude old faces

46

I know I am the seed
that has made you cry the most.
Yet, I still strive to give you reasons
to brag and boast.
It is such a blessing to have
you here for yet another year.
Though physically far,
I still keep you near.
I will never forget
the things you taught me.
Some say a woman can't raise
a man, but you raised 2.
You often tell us you are proud of us,
and Mama, you should know that
we are proud of you too.
You are beautiful, and we appreciate
everything you've done and all that you do.
On this day and every day,
I will always love you.

When I Think of Her

When I think of her, I wonder
how can I be better to become
the man she deserves.
How can I impress her with
the way I combine these words?
How can I love her
the way that she loves me?
How can I assure her that
I want this l-o-v-e?
Every day, she inspires me
and motivates me to succeed.
I can not lie. I want her to carry my seed.
She believes in me
more than I believe in myself.
She cares about my strength.
She cares about my health.
She has shown me a love similar
to the love my mother gives.
When I think of her,
I just want to live.

A Poem for Her

Cheer up because you're beautiful,
and you have so many reasons to smile.
Cheer up because you rock,
and you make others smile.
Cheer up because you're gorgeous,
and you are an awesome mother.
You're all that and a bag of chips
in my eyes and your brothers'.
You're bright like a star.
Star is your middle name.
You've given me moments to cherish
through conversation and games.
Your smile lifts me up.
With you, I feel strong.
In your love and care
is where I feel my heart
belongs.

Failure Is Not An Option

Failure is not an option.
You can take that however you choose.
We all want to be winners,
but at times, we all lose.
Truth is based on fact,
which is what can be proved.
We all have a gift,
something that we love to do,
maybe even something that
you love more than you…
Our gift is from our Heavenly Father,
and we should use our gift for good.
Our gift provides understanding
when we seem to be misunderstood.

Stages of Infatuation

Her voice touches my soul. Her words make me feel free.
Each time I arrive in her presence, I realize that is where I want to be.
She makes me want to travel the world.
She encourages me to try new things.
I real deal want to be her Black King, and she can be my Puerto Rican Queen.
I love when she says, "Roll Tide." Her voice is sweet and silky smooth.
She loves the way I walk and talk, and the fact that I am so cool.
I love that she is full of love, life, and laughter.
She makes me want to turn the page, chapter after chapter.

Only Human

I never said things to you
out of anger that I didn't mean
because even in those times,
I know that I have love for you.
But yes, I said some cold things.
I've done some cold things.
I've had some cold dreams.
I never tried to be perfect.
I never wanted to be.
And, you thought so highly of me
that you forgot to see the man in me.

A Stare-down With Hatred

You say I walked in like I got a chip on my shoulder.
Yeah, you're right.
You ain't been through what my people been through
in life, the everyday fight
...the thousands of years of changing our history from
black to white
If it was up to you, I'm sure you would have killed us
all long ago.
Now I'm up like an early bird, and I plan to stay woke.

Human Imperfection

Imperfect beings we are, and things in life happen beyond our control.

We go through ups and downs as life tends to unfold.

Life is still precious no matter the obstacles we face.

Until we are dead and gone, we must continue to race.

Searching for Peace

I tried to do things the right way,
but I tried for the wrong reasons.
Now, I've been going through this storm
for the past four seasons.
Angels and demons…
I have seen it all.
To find true happiness,
I will risk it all.

Dreams, Intuition, & Reality

We have dreams that we want to ignore.

Things happen that shake us to the core.

You set expectations high,

and people often let you down.

I let people down too.

What goes around comes around.

Even if You Never

Even if you never speak to me again, I'll love you.
If I never talk to you again, in my mind, I'll hug you.
If I can never feel your lips,
nor make love to you ever again,
I will reminisce of those times over and over again.
Even if I can never hold your hand again,
I will still love you as a lover and a friend.
If I can never hold you again, nor rock you to sleep,
I will remember the times you laid upon my heartbeat.
Even if I can never cook for you, nor feed you ever again,
I will smile for those times when I did.
If I can never see you again,
I will still ask myself when can I see you again.
Even if you never speak to me again, I'll love you.
If I never touch you again, in my mind, I'll hug you.
If I can never be in your presence ever again,
I will still love you as a lover and a friend.

Still Shedding Tears

I'm still shedding tears for you.

I'm still laughing at the hilarious memories you've given me.

I'm still expressing my fears to you.

I thank you for loving and strengthening me.

I'm still shedding tears for you.

I'm still missing your every expression.

I'm still shedding tears. I'm still shedding tears.

Every situation is a beautiful lesson.

I'm still shedding tears for you.

And, I know you'll smile even through the pain.

When the sun is behind the clouds, and the clouds are dark,

you will still shine even if it rains.

I'm still shedding tears for you because

you are so far beyond amazing.

My heart is still full of love for you,

a love that is burning and blazing.

Questions

I find myself asking:

Who is texting you good morning now?

Who is making your day and telling you goodnight?

Who will come along and do everything right?

Who is going to love you?

Who is going to hold you?

Who will give you their all the way I was supposed to?

Who is going to give you their son?

Who is going to come along and be that special one?

Who is going to love you better than I did?

Who is the special person that will

give you multiple kids?

Who will hold your hand?

On whose chest will you lay?

Who will come along and make your day?

Love, Remorse, & Bad Decisions

I'll understand if you hate me.
I will never get over you.
I might never forgive myself
for what I put you through.
You deserve so much better.
I pray that he finds you.
Of me, I hope that
he never reminds you.

The Realest Love

Have you ever fallen in love with a person
you didn't know?
Not knowing if you would ever see where things could go
Have you ever fell in love with the way a person walked,
the way she smelled, the way she talked?
Have you ever fell in love with a person
when you heard her speak,
when your back was turned, her face you couldn't see?
Have you ever fell in love with a person
for their kindness and grace?
You get close to her and your heart begins to race
Have you ever fell in love with a person's hair?
A person with whom you would gladly share your air.

Ending

You're over me now.
I'm nothing to you.
I screwed up again,
but that's nothing new.

True Happiness

Happiness is not an event.

Your happiness should not be based on someone else.

Happiness is a decision that you must choose for yourself.

Happiness is an emotion that we fail

to control based upon situations,

but I believe we can choose happiness

in many things we are facing.

Happiness is a jewel that we must hold tight.

We can choose to be happy in the day and the night.

I have not always been happy,

but I choose to be happy now.

I have spent too much of my life without a smile

and with a frown.

Happiness is a feeling that we all want to feel.

You must choose to be happy if I must keep it real.

Year 27

27 years, still look 19
I will follow you barefoot,
in Jordans, or Nikes.
For every punch, every slap,
every kick, and every scream,
there is no other man I'd rather have
on my team.
I believe in you when
no one else will do.
I will do for you what
no one else will do.
I love you to the moon,
beyond, and back.
I am your keeper, and I
will carry you
upon my back.

War Within

Everyday, I put on my cape
and walk through life
as if it is all sunny and bright.
But, on the inside, it's dark.
My mind never rests,
and I can't sleep at night.

A Rock & A Hard Place

I fell in love with a woman who wasn't mine.
Sadly, I allowed myself not to stay.
I am still not in love with the woman who is mine,
and I do not want to live this way.

Simple Honesty

I knew when we got off the phone
that you would not call back.
Just be real with me…
no half-truths, no acts.

Can We?

Can we start over?
Can we take it slow?
I believe there are no limits
to how far we can go.
Can we go back there
to the same place again?
Can I be your lover after
I am first your friend?
Can I kiss your sweet lips?
Can I hold your hand?
Can I protect you?
Can I be your man?

Cowards with Badges

Words mean nothing when the actions don't align.
It's those who look like me constantly
being shot in the spine.
Black and Beautiful,
but we are treated like we are nothing
in this so-called land of the free.
Yet, you call us savages when we turn to the streets.
But, savage is when you shoot a man
in the back seven times.
He has no eyes in the back of his head,
so when you decided to
pull that trigger, he was basically blind.
You shoot blind men, and you even kill our beautiful
black boys and girls.
So, I understood Tupac when he said
"F--- the world."
And, I felt J. Cole when he said he came fast like
9-1-1 in white neighborhoods.
Cause 9-1-1 might shoot you for any reason
if you were born, raised, or live in
a black neighborhood.

I'm Not Who You Thought I Was

I'm not who you thought I was.
Because I was squared away,
you thought that I was goody two shoes
and that I would turn my back on
those who needed me the most.
I'm not who you thought I was.
I saw the way you looked when you walked by. I
heard what you said, and the word came to me
that there was an angel nearby who was actually
the devil in disguise.
I'm not who you thought I was.
Your position is not enough.
Your power is not enough
Because I am protected by
the Most High who rests in the sky.

If I Could I Would

If I could take away the two years
of hurt I've caused you
and give you the happiness
I've experienced
in my 26 years of life,
I'd do it in a heartbeat.
If I could go back to the day
before I met you,
I never would have met you.
At least, that way,
I never would have hurt you.
I never should have lied to you
when all you wanted was my truth.
I was a coward.
I was a liar, and
I was a fool too.

Tough Feelings

Sometimes, I want to cry,
but my tears are dry.
Sometimes, I want to cry,
but I don't know why.
Sometimes, I want to cry,
but my pride won't let me.
Sometimes, I want to cry
and be high like when
the trees be…shhh.
Sometimes, I want to cry,
but I tell myself I'm too strong.
Sometimes, I want to cry
because I wish that I never
left home.
Sometimes, I want to cry
and long for a shoulder to lean on.
But rarely do I cry because
rarely do I pick up the phone.

Pain & Poetry

I'm feeling like Rod Wave.
All I got is pain and poetry
that's gone put you in your feelings.
I am sick of injustice.
I am sick of these killings.
Peaceful, but rugged...
so misunderstood.
You cannot treat us badly
and expect us to be good.
It's a new form of slavery,
and many don't see that.
Others are aware but will not
publicly admit that.
I am serving my country,
and my country is steady
killing those who look like me.
I am serving my country,
and my country is steady
murdering us.
Would you prefer my words,
or would you rather me put
my guns and my fists up?

Clever Deceit

Got a lot on my chest,
and my plate is full.
When my desires are unfulfilled,
it's away I pull.
Silently and cleverly,
I isolate to the max.
When I shake feelings for you,
you will never get them back.
They say if you play with fire
you will get burned.
We've all been played.
And, if you feel you haven't,
just wait for your turn.

If You Knew What It Was Like to Be Black

If you knew what it was like to be black,
would you say the things that you say?
Would you still smile in my face
and call me something foul
the moment I walked away?
If you knew what it was like to be black,
would you want to be hated
for the color of your skin?
Well, these are things I face
because of the skin I'm in.
If you knew what it was like to be black,
would you try to hide your cold hate?
If you knew that I felt it in your vibe
when you walked by?
If you knew that I could see it in your face?

Cold Shoulder

Men play games that women play better.
They'll make you pull down your beanie
and tuck in your sweater.
It's a cold day outside, and I just want to stay in.
I don't want to be hurt like this ever again.

Breaking Bad Habits

It's like I'm learning how
to be faithful all over again.
Never that I wanted to be
unfaithful from the begin...
yet, I found myself
in a tough situation.
I made one bad decision,
and then I continued to make it.
I was verbally abused
and not appreciated.
I then verbally abused
and showed no appreciation.
See, we would not speak for days
and then have the dopest of sex.
But in the name of love,
even the dopest of sex is just not enough.
So, yes, I'm learning how to be
faithful all over again.
And this time, I will be faithful
from beginning to end.

Reality

You no longer have faith in me.

You no longer feel the same way.

I am not ok today, but I will be ok.

You no longer feel the same way.

You no longer desire to be my wife.

I am not ok today, but I will be alright.

Heartbreak on the Rise

I really don't want to move on,
but I refuse to sit here and wait
for my heart to be broken
all over again.
I never thought that I would
become your lover,
but I always knew that
I wanted to be more than
just your friend.
Now, we are in a tough place,
and we have no clue
where things will go.
I see now that I love you
way more than I thought I did
and that we truly reap everything
that we sow.

Phases of Love

Love is a beautiful thing.
Yet, love is a dangerous game.
Love is full of joy and laughter,
but also heartache and pain.
Love is full of endless possibilities
and full of possibilities that end.
Love is a mystery that I cannot explain.
When will my heartbreak end?

Reaping

Not everything that happens is meant
to be understood by all.
Even if we're not still tight, I still have love
for those I ever considered to be my dawg.
For every choice we make, we will pay the price,
whether lying, stealing, or sneaking and laying pipe.

Queen's Reign

You're a Queen, and you should never
suppress who you are when you are
around others.
That also goes for the rest of y'all
sisters and brothers.
You should never worry about
how people will feel
when you're just being real.
Respect is a must, and kindness kills.
You're a Queen, and you should never
dim your light to make others feel bright.
Shine like when your King kisses your forehead
and tucks you in at night.

Warring One

I haven't been the same since I came home.
It's not like I was in a combat zone, but
the way I see it, my whole life has been a combat zone.
Who can I count on the most when I am weak?
Me, myself, and I, The Messiah, and The Most High
Cause everyone else is going to let you down
Everyone else will say screw it when they see
how ugly you are on the inside.
Everyone else is going to run and hide when they see
that monster that is on the inside.
Please don't feel sorry. Please show me no pity
because even when I want to cry, my tears are dry.
And, I am still mean, aggressive, and gritty.
I'm like the villain in the horror movie.
My smile is cunning, and my attributes
are really my flaws viewed optimistically.

Move Forward

Stop blaming yourself for all the things that went wrong.
Stop blaming yourself for when you reached out,
and that person chose not to pick up the phone.
Stop beating yourself up for all the mistakes
and bad decisions you made.
Forgive yourself for all the games you played.
Stop telling yourself that no one will ever love you
the way you want to be loved.
Stop believing that no one will grind
as hard for you as you do for others.
Stop believing that he or she is the only person
that can make you feel a certain way.
Remind yourself that there was a new opportunity
when you woke up today.
Stop holding on to everything that
traumatized you in the past.
Everything has its season, and
not every good thing was built to last.
Stop running from the truth.
Stop being so afraid of something new.
Time heals all wounds when the time is due.

Poetry & Rhyme

I keep saying I'm going to call you, and I haven't called
yet.
You could recite poetry to me all day,
and I would never break a sweat.
When I see you on your pole, you give me so much life.
You dance and twirl in your own world
as if you know everything will be alright.
When I see you on your pole, you make me
want to pull up and spend my whole stimulus check
...as I sit back and watch while
my heart attempts to penetrate my chest.
Your voice is like a magnitude of beautiful, poetic
vibrations,
A thrill that inspires, motivates, and leaves my mind
racing.
When I see you on your pole, I laugh and smile.
So, I had to let you know that I'm digging your style.
No makeup, no lipstick, afro puff to the side.
A Boyz N The Hood t-shirt
with Doughboy kicked back
leaning on his ride.

What It Is

What is access?

What is confusion?

Is love as sweet as some say?

Or, is it just an allusion?

The Coldest Weather

I lay on my side and pretend like I am holding you.

Yet, you do not want me anymore.

I knew I was having a breakdown last night

as I was crying and pacing across the floor.

Here I am in my weakest moments.

I cannot sleep. I am battling depression.

All I want is to hear your voice,

hold you, and have you next to me.

But, life goes on, and I must move on.

Feelings change and people too.

Though they fade, memories last forever.

My heart is broken, and this is the coldest weather.

Wrath Is Cruel

They say it's hard to separate the real from the fake,
and that's why I stay in my lane.
You'd be surprised at those who will
slander your name all for their personal gain.
You'd be surprised at those who will
slander your name even when they have nothing to gain.
Slandering one's name will yield no gain,
only self-inflicted pain.

Distant Love

Loving you from a distance is not easy.
Yet, the thought of being without you
is even harder than that.
You make me smile even when I'm angry
and even when you've said things
that hurt my feelings.
Yes, even when you've said things
that hurt my feelings.
Despite all we've been through,
I still believe that you are the one for me.
There is no other woman that I want
to give my time to.
I only want to give my effort to you.
I laugh so often when I think
of memories that we created.
I feel this way for now, but soon,
I will be completely elevated.

Proud Loner

I never met a person that I needed
more than I needed myself.
I will grind and take care of mine
until the time I breathe my last breath.
The world is often a cold place.
Most people want something for nothing.
Cross me, and I boss up every time.
In no way, shape, or fashion, am I bluffing.
Intellectuals move in a different way.
With silence and kindness, we slay.
Yet, we can still get gritty like DMX.
Don't try your luck. Don't play.
I'm on to something different,
so, I move differently.
Without a single weapon will I face
every single one of my enemies.
It is not my time until it is my time.
Therefore, I stress about no one finishing me.
Water is swift. Wind moves with grace.
I make love to the page.
The page is my ace.

Regal Flow

Maybe, I'm stuck in time,
an old soul, but in my prime.
I've seen 25s on 10 scales,
so, it's no longer enough
if you are a dime.
I'm more interested in your mind,
not how you look physically.
Even if you're thick with nice lips,
that might have been enough
when I was 17.
Walk like an Emperor.
Move like a boss.
Been plotted on since day one
Ain't ever been crossed

Red Flame

More gorgeous than a model
A model you are.
I replayed the way you said bye
as I walked to my car.
Was it a sign of interest?
Were you just being kind?
Ever since the last time,
you've been running through my mind.
A dress so fitting with the boldest curves
I walked past you with effort
trying to calm my nerves.
You smiled. I smiled.
It was oh so kind.
Natascha, I must say
that you are oh so fine.
Eyebrows impeccable,
as smooth as wine
Natascha, I must say
that you are oh so fine.

What Would be Different?

What would be different if you were mine?
I'd give you flowers, hugs,
and kisses all the time.
I would be your Mister.
You would be my Misses.
I would till the yard while
you washed the dishes.
We would cook, clean,
and play games all day.
We would tease one another
as we bypassed in the hallway.
Maybe, forever we will remain friends,
but maybe, this is where we begin again.

I Choose You

I think about you in ways that friends
don't think about friends.
It's been nearly two years.
Yet, I still don't want things to end.
I want deeply to be yours and you to be mine.
I will give you my love. I will give you my time.
I will make love to you forever and always.
I will build you up and support you in all ways.
I will hold your hands. I will comb your hair.
If it was to save you, I would give you my air.
My love for you is deeper than I know how to explain.
I love you through all hurt. I love you through all pain.
I ask your forgiveness for everything I did wrong.
May I take your hand and play you a love song?
Let me hold and rock you the way I used to.
I'll give you everything I used to
multiplied with something new.
I will love your children as if they are mine.
I will choose you until the end of time.

Reminiscing It All

Sometimes, I hate how much I love you.
And, it's not that I have ill feelings towards you.
It's simply that I don't understand why I feel
so strongly for you after all this time,
and it bothers me.
I hate all of the pain that I caused you.
I hate all of the pain that you caused me.
I hate every bad thing that happened between us.
I wish it was like a bad dream;
you wake up, and it's over.
But, unfortunately that's not how life works.

A Butterfly In The Wind

I'm slowly vanishing
into a more intellectual me,
truthfully getting deeper
like the depths of the sea.
My mind is expanding.
For knowledge, it's demanding.
And, my brain is like a heaven
for metaphors and similes.

Fine Brass

Every time I look at the sky, I wonder if the Most High has locks like those described in Song of Solomon 5:11. Or, if He has a 360-wave pattern like the Israelites on the ancient Hebrew hieroglyphs. When I read the verses that describe the Ancient of Days' skin being like unto fine brass, I always come to the same conclusion about Yeshua Ha'Massiach. Every time I look in the mirror, I see fine brass. Every time I look at my daughters, I see fine brass. Every time I look at my family, I see fine brass.

About the Author

Martinez Shaver is an inspirational speaker, podcaster, author, soldier, and resilience trainer. He published his first collection of poetry, Thoughts of A Cool Guy, at the age of 21. A Butterfly In The Wind is his second of many more to come. Whether writing, serving in the field, or speaking on stage, he is the true embodiment of discipline, resilience, and leadership. Martinez empowers audiences to achieve success that can only come through hard work, quality decisions, good faith, and strong character. Because he understands the power of positive community and authentic storytelling, he fervidly shares his journey of overcoming self- sabotage, facing adversity, and choosing a better life and future despite the odds.